Theodore in November

by Natalie Williams

(JM)

JEREMY MILLS
PUBLISHING LIMITED

Published by Jeremy Mills Publishing Limited
www.jeremymillspublishing.co.uk

First Published 2009
Text © Natalie Williams

ISBN 978-1-906600-10-5

To Margaret Vickery, who has known
both joy and sadness in her life
and has taught me the value of both.

I love you the most.

Table of Contents

Foreword

This was my first long poetic work, and in a lot of ways has been as much of a journey for me to write as the main character Theodore embarks upon.

The expression 'Theodore in November' is entirely symbolic, but it's meant to be entirely not obvious. Since it symbolizes love in its true form it cannot, in my opinion, be easily understood.

Theodore is true love's fight to discover itself, and in some ways is undiscovered. It is an ideal that becomes tainted by experience but then matured by it.

November, to me, is a middle time between some place, between winter, summer and autumn; a metaphor for an Eden, an undiscovered country.

Into these poems I have poured my own experiences of love, of Theodore as it were, along with my own journey to November and in a somewhat amusing way I have complete ownership of all life's little idiosyncrasies that leap from the pages of the discoveries made.

A poetic journey to Eden, to November.

Natalie Williams

Theodore In November

Once there
Being A
Theodore named
Of Destiny
Of Rapture
Of melodies shamed
Stood to gain
In September rain
Theodore gathered pain
Since September
Was in heart distemper
Since he longed for sweet November
Fast forwarded become
Theodore became undone
And set forth words free
Wrote Love's own thoughts
This the journey's journal
From September to November sought

Sweet Tomorrow

Every part of me reaches out to you
Because I need you, I bleed for you
And my sorrow aches for that sweet tomorrow
When I can be burned by your touch
For you I love so much
My lips open parted, soft hand warmed
Reach out to kiss you
I miss you …

My hands reach out to thread through your hair
But all I reach is thin air
You are not there …

My skin cries out to be moving under you
I am in wonder
Of you
I long to drink my fill
But all I see is wind blowing out my window sill

And so I send my heart to you in winds blowing
They hush to you
With my message going

My eyes are weary
Tired with no sight of you
Forgotten daylight of you
Filled with delights of worlds and stars studded
But with no frame of you budded

My heart beats in an undertone
Take me home

For my life has past
Take me where all dark is out
And lights are in
Take me
Within
You are my midnight opal
Multicolour in my completeness
For desire for your sweetness

So much I feel
I touch you with my never-ending love and unashamed begging
I feel my solidity in this moment ebbing
Phased out and Translocated
I must have my ache for you
Sated

Sweet pink fancies creamed to the brink
My lusty passions are more than even I can think
I must drink
You
Incomplete and empty
I must be made whole by you
Fill my ears with your living
Ellipse my melody
As music on a page
Place high notes to my low
Take me where you go

So linked I feel
I now feel unreal
In present now
I know not how
Every part reaches, can you feel me

Cinnamon Lover

Me oh my
I feel kinda spinning
Kinda shy
Like a butterfly
Trapped in a wheeze
Of a moment's sweet tease
Feel like dropping to knees
To beg pretty please

Feel kinda passed by
Feel like I should cry
Or want to die
But I'm turning into you
Don't know
Can't grow
Out of the moment
That I loved you

I don't feel like I'm winning
I'm sure this is a game
But I'm getting out of breath
When I hear your name

Feel like my hearts panting
With cinnamon ranting
This feels otherworldly
Or some compromise
A reprieve to see into your eyes
Just when I drop my disguise
I am lost without you

Cover Me In Latin

Easy lover
My body cover
With your sweat in love
Encase my skin like a glove
Consume me, and then exhume me
Petrified with this love lust love
Cross stitched, got an itch up above
Stained, pained, tortured twisty
My eyes are misty
Wistful
Theodore, or some such name
Heart I blame
Torched and gazing
All guns blazing
Scratched and bleeding
I'm feeding

Easy lover
Put me in a corner
On a wall
Stretch me into times and future past
Make this last
Lengthen me
Strengthen me
Place me in a photo frame
Don't tell me it's a game
I'm feeling your name
Spelling out the letters
With each crescendo
The moments in your eyes
In your life
In my cries

Easy lover
I'm skinned by you
And gift wrapped in joy
Present me to your finest woes
And I shall curl my toes
Tie me up in bows
Let's not come to blows
See how this playtime goes

Easy lover
Heart of mine
I'm spent
Looking for a vent
Wish to be touched by you
Feel so much for you
Rising inside like a lava experience
Kiss me at your convenience

It's just too long
I'm losing my strong
Choosing to tag along
Cos this doesn't feel wrong
I'm written in lyrical splendour
And sold to a vendor
And restored
Unexplored
Covered in Latin
Naked me in satin

Guinevere's Kiss

Guinevere's kiss
This must be what bliss
Feels like

Torture, it seems like torture
Exploded
I feel so scolded

Understanding this seems so impossible
Impassable to see what has been done
My moody madness seems just fun
To you

Sweet like ivory, words cannot express
How much of a mess
I am in this dress
Sewn with your kisses
And draped with your dreams
Flowing like silky streams
You still me

Betraying all inner demons
You cannot fail me
You cannot avail me
Guinevere

Pale like the inner soul of a flower
I cannot see into you
Though I stare
You disappear
You are not there

And begging with all life I feel
I beg for you to just be real
Guinevere
My love

Token, the breath of sweet mist
This is the moment of Guinevere's kiss

Naïve
Unattended
So stupid
In love.

Natalie Williams

Love Bliss

In your eyes I see
Or is it just me
You dance through life so sexily
Or is it just me
I feel all out of sync
Haven't touched a drink
Just don't get what this is
Could this be love bliss?
And when we kiss
I feel a near miss
To heaven or another plane
Like I'm lost in tropical rain

You seem exposed
This love I'm shown
You seem fearful, and explored
And surprisingly, I'm not bored
You touch me, my heart races
It jumps in leaps and bounding paces
Burnt where your hands were
Heated where your lips were

Who are you?
Secret
You aren't a rhyming couplet
Or some summer view
You fill my cheeks with a red hue
But I'm so practised at hiding
And time biding
And man riding

9

Don't set me off
Topple me off this confidence
I was settled then
Settled with many men

But this desire
And a tiny voice that seems so loud
Would do many a mother proud
Speaking volumes, seems so cliché
But you surprised me today
Shaken up
I'd given up

Confusion

Natalie Williams

Words Of Wine

Bettered by the touch of you
Just feel so much for you
Improved like the finest wine
I become it, because you're mine
To look into your eyes simple
And for that I long
And I repeat my last vision
A thousand times over
Just to see you lover
You mature me
You add the spice
You pull me out
Make me silent when I could shout
But I smile in my soul
Even angered, because I'm with you
Challenge me, you are challenging
I can feel my muscles tightening
They ache to be near you
Anything of me is seared by you
Branded, bottled, capsized by you
You shatter all false and naked safety
And I am liquid in your hands
Liquid to fulfil your demands
Flow to meet your commands
You drink me up yet I am drunk with you
River of your blood, I feel
What it's like to be you
Inside you, I hide you
Hide you from another's view
You are all I am, and do
To you I'm true

Box me for a thousand years, drink me still
All I am will fulfil your will.

Go To Sleep While
I Make Love To You

Memory
Heartbroken
In the eyes of sorrowed dreams
Penetrate ungainly sunbeams
In the soul
A mirrored foe
Tied up
Screwed up
With a mere madness bow
What a feeling
Head forward
Reeling
Spinning
Onto the forehead of time pinning
A word
A sentence shattered
Splintered forth into a million pictures
Moments could be fractures
Days squinted into weeks
Watery emotions in bucket of tears leaks
Captured
Imprisoned
So sweet it hurts
Painful
Worshipped and adored
Theodored
Grabbed my soul
And taken to another place
Where all people and memories fade

And in nothingness, in black clouds we wade
This is our face
Earth we replace
With solar showers
And planets borne
Star studded
Hearts thudded
Shoot forth loveliness
To replace loneliness colour in your eyes
Past dies
Lost in a moment

Warm And Fuzzy Feeling

You have a beauty that isn't often seen
You're the beauty that's a fading memory
Of a dream
As you wake to dawn
You're a sunset born
You're the beauty of a lonely swan
In a deserted lake
By moonlit fire-night
On the 15th September
You're the beauty not many remember
And no one forgets
You're the beauty of crazy high stake bets
You're the beauty of your reflection
As water meets in convection
After a rain storm
You're the beauty of 'never again' strength sworn
You're the beauty of Christmas morning
You're the beauty of the realisation
that you're up on the budget dawning
You're the beauty of sharing that last crisp
You're the taste of prawn cocktail
With peanuts and beer
And the best pub you've ever been to discovered
When with a flat tyre
Off the road you veer
You're the smell of just rightly done steak
You're the sound of a thousand loves to make
You're the cliché
You're what makes girls giggle
You're the beauty of the best ass in the world wiggle
You're the smell of a new Ferrari

You're the beauty in the heart-warming
Hug of a feeling
Of that first sorry
You're what's ok
What's right
You're the man I turn to look at
To stare at
To wonder at
When I can't sleep at night.

Unlikely Perfection

Well this is a jump
Never jump
Not least with eyes open
Certainly not with heart broken

Unlikely perfection
You taste ... mmm
Moan
Like a sweet confection
Savoury or unsavoury
Like an inverted melancholy

Guess I mixed up my happy pill
Cause here I am breathing silence into your window sill
Making names with my finger
Theodore, let your moist linger

Not sure what it is I taste
But I like it
Minty with just a hint
Oh no
Nothing to declare
Keep my hands on the desk, the defence rests
'Aint answering no questions
Love loving you, oh no
Happy to let you go, no
I'm just staring to see the dreams you're wearing
Smile and wave
Like daddy at sports day
I like to see you blossom away
Though I don't know

What flower you'll grow
Or whether you'll seed
Whether I'll make you bleed
Sighing unlikely perfection
Finger ceased in cessation
As I stare
At letter O
As I hear you open my door
You seem more comfortable than before

Say my name, I shiver
And my index finger is all quiver, then
suddenly
And peculiarly
Your hand on mine
My skin seems meant for you

Back to continuous thought
You lead me, though I've not sought
Want to feed me
Do you Theodore?
As I turn into laughter
Just to close the door that little bit harder
I'm heart stopped
Eyelashes dropped
Your names been completed
as I retreated
by some mysterious convection

Theodore

And a visitor's outlined
As you wait behind
What you are, what confection
Of unlikely perfection

Natalie Williams

Take Me Back To November

Take me back to November
Make me remember
The steps I took to December

Develop me
Envelop me
Play with me
Today with me
Stay
with me

Write me into pentameter
Write me into verse
Speak me, then breathe my life back into you
Reverse

Follow me
Hollow me out
Stroke me into grains of sand
Sell me, profit from me
Then deny my supply
Deny my demand

Blow me into a rainbow
Fly me like a kite
Let me be the moonlight
On a November night

Paint me with words that don't rhyme
Let me do time
Let me be jailed by you

Nailed by you
Brush me into a moment
Rush me like a component

Put me together
Then rip me apart
Turn me into September
Then unbreak my heart

Let me be the breath you repel
And the oxygen you expel
Sing me into a bird
Measure me with just one word

Give me feathers
Tie me up in leathers
Dominate me
And I'll slap you in verse
So make me adverse
Unbalance me
Checkmate my thoughts
Make me out of sorts

Melody me as melodies sung
Sweep me along
Try to keep me strong
Make me short when I'm long

Support me then break me down
Take my tiara, then give me a crown
Cut me into a four-pointed star
Then throw me afar
Make me the beginning of a conclusion
Take me into mathematical solution

Solve me with seclusion
Slip me in your drink
Let me ride the petals of your heavy metals
Kiss the flutters of your eyelashes as you blink

Make me into a five course meal
Change me to what you feel
Make, unmake me real

Let me be the mirror
Of all things unseen
Take me back to November
To where I've once been
Let me the crack of light
Seeping through your heart door
Let me be your before

Coronate me
When I blow you a frown
Swap places with me
Let me be your tomorrow
Your glacial brown

Liquidate me
Annotate me
Reiterate me
Spin sate me
Sex me
Anorex my emotion
Take a vow
Let me be the furrow in your baby brow

Mother me
And absorb my unsung heroes

Wipe me with details
Blackboard chalk, be my unborn child
Make me soppy when I'm mild

Take my two faces
Take me places
Take me through my paces
Untie my laces
And make me trip
Make me take a naked dip
Into the pool of November
Reveal my distemper
Make me remember

Play Me Like A Harp

Silence speaks in volumes
It's not what I can say
Your body tears mixed with mine
They cry out for me
Sigh out on me
Don't die out on me
I groan their name
In answered moan
They grab me closer
Until I ache
Until I am shattering
Until I almost break
'Must be filled' I utter
'One moment, wait' they mutter
Heat breathes life into me
Until no words are left unsaid
And sweet kisses on soft skin form my bed
Hair becomes like silk
Mind forgets
Tongue wetting lightly
On my begging neck
It seems the sun has set
A moment of silence
As into your eyes I stare
Licking my lips
I am your harp
So play me Theodore
Though you've not had lessons
I can play the sweetest arias
Until old times are ended
And past and future

With present are bended
Play me well
And your November will be mended
I speak with eyes this spell
Sigh spell
My name
I am Harbringer of old
Harbringer with her harp of fame

Natalie Williams

Dorothy

Angels singing, mouths open
Wide with jewels of sound
Crashing, thudding
Their eyes hit the ground
Wings touch my soul
Eclipsed and entwined
What once a half, now seems a whole
Follow me if you must
Dorothy's in Oz I'm guessing
Must have those angels stressing
Just to make me a believer
They found me a golden retriever
Like to catch my bone
Doesn't seem to want to be alone
Memories play like hands on a harp
With each strum a different melody
Projecting picture almost sounded
Winding back, reverse, play
Silence reaches me in uncomfortable glamour
Like a kiss followed by stammer
Heart sounds into an iron hammer
Angels' gaze
This is a love craze
Silence surrounding me
Silence surrounding you
Like angel's blanket
Muffled in ears
And in your eyes I see
You play our lives together through the years

Let Me Breathe In Your Today

Worship me from afar
I am aching
Breaking
Pitch and tar

Worship me, I am exclusive
I am resplendent
Independent
Make love to me reclusive

Worship me as worship goes
Suck in my woes
And no one knows
Where I go when I doze

Worship me, my trinkets lie
Come what may, come and play
Feel me breathe in your today
And blow out your summer bay

Worship me, thread me
Beadily
Draw me in and tie me closed
Speedily
Shiny smooth down my reflection
And mess me up with your convection

Tentative, this is Theodore unseen
What dreams may come
Glean from me
Through gropings must

Do not shower me
For I will rust

Nor bury me
Or expose me open
Or wind me too much
For I'll be broken

No is undone
These words affirmative
It's true we're close
That's confirmative

Slip Into Me

Slip into me
Into the void
I am your sunrise to avoid
I spin my joy for you, my ploy for you
Into verse
I am your abstract, your adverse

Slip into me
This is your sin to me
Where you've been to me
How you've seemed to me
What shall you say?
Will you ricochet these melting dreams away?

Truth stacking, lies lacking
In this diverse slip
Cauldron of promise and confusion
The fat's been skimmed by diffusion
Seems I am an abyss solution

Gypsy dreamer, Jester's believer
Lost all faith
Two pinches, maybe three
Peculiarly
Slip into me

Peppermint Defeat

Tantalising
I'm definitely fraternising
With this sodomy
Emotional cacophony
These words seem unwritten
Or unpromising, or forbidden
Seems I've ceased and faltered
Too fettered I've halted
Truth seems unrecognisable
The shadows are disguised
It just seems so late
Too late to unbend my fate
And promises are all broken
The door crack left open
Seems it slipped my mind
To turn to lock, to key to find
It seems a merry chase
Furrows guttered in my face
Of all lies I've sold
When love's murders gone cold
Fear slips in
Right in the within
Whirl winded I'm hindered
The return slow I've lingered
Hush like a lady
Until feelings are hazy
As she slips right on by
Stops old man Theodore asking why
With her woolly woolliness
She's clean cleanliness
Her feet are untravelled

Her hearts unravelled
But I'm sooty
But I'm sweet
Sweet like peppermint defeat
But I just feel cowardly lazy
To step out from the hazy
My skittish splendour
Olden times has rendered
It's just like Paddington's hat
Watching trains go by sat
My welcome mat
Uninviting, just for show
Tells tantalizing to go
Not on my own, words uttered
Not just bread I've buttered
I'm losing my mind's path
And invoking heart's wrath
Just won't do, this change reverse is a hue
A sullen snapshot
Lump throat, tied knot
Got me all exploded
Me oh my I'm unencoded
Just too tasty to linger
To watch in frozen silence
The door crack sneaks bigger.

Natalie Williams

Take Off My Sunshine Dress

Delegated
This desire
Graduated
Feel twisted, hit and miss
This sultry bliss
With the knock-knocking
I'm a tick-tocking
Like Alice and her clock
I'm about to do some dock-docking
Speedy
I'm developing greedy
Like a maiden flower
I'm exceeding in power
Elevated
Until I'm sated
It seems a sunshine dress
Has got me all in a mess
Must confess
These hidden lies
That form my disguise
Are words unwritten
Rhythm to sever
Usage not clever
Confusion and unusual
Let me create a visual
Of a drug so intoxicating
So melancholy it's self-deprecating
This is just one emotion
Caused by life in slow motion
Skin on skin
Pulsing within

And movement in frames
Murmuring of names
It's got me drinking dizzy
This is getting busy
Encased in plated flames
Painted in Theodore's shame
Uncomfortable colour
This unending cover
Beg for endless blossom
'Theodore, *mi Amore*'
She says, he says
'Take off my sunshine dress
Lets get ourselves in a mess'.

Natalie Williams

To Home

When I look at you,
I think of home.
Memories of twisted surf
and splashing cliffs.
Black rocks mottled with grey.
Splashes of organic paint.
Soot soul driven
by winds and hurricane.
Driving home in darkness.
Hot lemonade summers,
red with raspberries and cream.
What a lovely dream
it is to look at you.

When I think of you,
I look at home.
Coconut coloured eyes,
eyelashes lifting
and drooping
with shy.
Nude pink hills; your hips are
mountains I climb with fingered wishes,
and flowered lilac kisses.
When you smile secret ideas
lift with the lines your glasses
created.
End pecked on your nose
Chocolate threads your hair is knitted,
entertained by your wit.

When I look at home, I look at you.
I am there again.
With you.

Milky Gritted Stone

I look at you as if I would a stone, the prettiest kind.
In my mind, you are that stone.
Solid.
Black.
Light-hidden and drifted from waters on shore as I sit
half-wet,
half-cold,
half-staring.

The stone is hard in hand,
round and smooth, scented of forgotten things.
Milky grit; its colour captures all
attentions of moon and eyes,
as I hold you.
My Stone.

Swift In Cinnamon

I dreary dreamt a day. When sky hung crippled clear
and crisp. Unhinged was I, deranged, lost, forlorn.
Though I stared at a statue, a statue stared scorn.
Wished I then for madness; a love so dear.
At night, when I sighed into cover, covers rippled fraught
With fire and ice intermingled, danced I with love true.
He wore gold of princes, and I, my gown royal blue
Electric Summer lights with my love I sought.

When I blood sworn, blood driven and blood stained.
Bore I no malice to world, rage lust or melancholic mood,
tender. Wished I for no cease, only passions in ages gained
and so I gained deep colour, the more I bruised brood
My love and I through the ages have remained
And to other swift souls mingling-tingling in sweet nude.
Swift in cinnamon.

About the Author

Natalie Williams was born in 1981 of African-Irish descent, in the newly formed country of Zimbabwe on the purple carpeted Jacaranda Lane. Life was filled in her early years with Irish fairy tales written by her grandfather, and the inspirational imaginings of the world of Narnia and Grimms' Fairy Tales. In the inspiring world of Africa, she began her journey as a writer, winning an Honours award for her poem 'The Thicket and the Musgrove' at the age of nine. Years later, she now launches her first poetry collection, drawing on the inspirations of her life and imagination.

www.natalie-williams.com

www.ingramcontent.com/pod-product-compliance
Lightning Source LLC
Chambersburg PA
CBHW060429090426
42734CB00011B/2498